Raise Successful Kids

The Importance of AMBTION in

Raising a CHAMPION

Copyright

Table of Contents

Introduction

I want to salute and thank you for downloading the book, "Raise Successful Kids".

This book contains proven strategies and steps on how to bring up an ambitious child with positive values and discipline. Also, the book informs you on good parenting and how you could improve your child's brain cognition effortlessly. However, parenting alone cannot be attributed to the main influence of a child's ambition. There are other external factors such as intellectual, social-emotional and academic development that significantly influence a child's ambition. These factors are beyond the parents' control

It is, therefore, important for every parent to be conversant with the relevant techniques of handling their child's ambition and emotions. That is what is exclusively offered to the readers of this book. You are equipped with skills that bring out the best in you in terms of parenthood.

Remember that a child who is intelligent but with no ambition is similar to a bird without wings. A child's interests, talents and passion should set the expectations but not giving the obligation to stereotypes. Therefore, it is important to nurture your child's ambition in the right way.

We salute you again for downloading this book. Enjoy reading it!

Chapter 1: Checking behavioral patterns in children

With time, the change in your child's behavioral pattern is inevitable, and it is of paramount importance to understand that the change is normal. The changes often result in various situations and events and as a parent, it is important to refrain from making prompt reactions to your child's behavioral changes. In this chapter, we take a look at the different ways in which you could cope and adapt to these changes; respond to the behavioral patterns; and understand your child's changes in behavioral patterns that seem dramatic.

It is vital to acknowledge that the behavioral changes will affect how you parent your child, their interactions with their peers and people in other social settings. It is recommended that you keep a close eye to your child's behavioral patterns and monitor their coping techniques in different situations. This is because how your child displays their pattern of behavior will have an impact not only on them but also those around them.

It is easy to monitor your child's behavior by simply applying authoritative or assertive democratic parenting style. To meet your child's needs in an appropriate and correct manner, it is advised that you adjust your parenting styles. However, that does not imply that you should be extremely permissive as a parent. Allowing your child considerate flexibility and freedom to say and act as they so desire has a little inclination in monitoring their behavior. It could make you blissfully unaware of your kid's regular developments, changes and patterns of behavior. Also, it is not healthy to be an over-strict parent.

Parenting styles provide guidance on how to handle your child's patterns of behavior. Also, they can be used to discover and understand the various reasons responsible for changes in their behavioral patterns. Good parenting styles guarantees a positive effect or impact on the child's behavioral pattern changes. Neglectful and negative parenting styles subjects the child to negative changes due to lack of proper monitoring.

Significantly, checking on your child's behavioral patterns enables them to; understand the changes in their behaviors; understand their feelings towards certain situations; understand how they can cope with the situations. This is why keeping a close look to your kid's behavior is essential and mandatory. It helps them to unravel both physical and emotional issues that have a heavy impact on their behaviors.

Behavioral Patterns

Causes of Changes in Behavioral Patterns

There are certain factors that affect the behavioral patterns in children such as changes in the family unit or at school, growing up, peer pressure or even trying to find their feet. Also, allowing children too much flexibility and freedom may subject them to uncontrollable behavioral patterns. The changes in behavioral patterns can be frustrating and confusing and, therefore, parents should identify and apply significant adjustments to deal with them.

Preventing Unruly Behavioral Patterns

Parents are advised to practice strategies that curb unaccepted behavioral patterns in their children. Some of these strategies include:

- ✓ Avoiding idleness in their children by keeping them occupied
- ✓ Concentrating their child's attention to positive things
- ✓ Having behavioral-based discussions with their child
- ✓ Incorporating rewards for good behavior
- ✓ Getting rid of unnecessary and unhealthy privileges

Dealing with Unacceptable Behavior

It is crucial to put in place certain strategies to tackle hurtful behavior changes in your child. Some of these strategies are mentioned below:

- Telling and explaining to the child why it is wrong

- Supporting the hurt child

- Instead of condemning your child, correct them for their unacceptable behavior

Commend your child for their acceptable behaviors

You can read more from:

http://www.education.com/reference/article/children-emotional-behavioral-disorders/

http://www.sensory-processing-disorder.com/behavior-problems-in-children.html

Chapter 2: Recognizing children's skills and talent early on

Recognizing in your child a budding talent is one of the best rewarding parts of parenthood. Parents can play a significant role in exploring their child's creativity that comes naturally during childhood. However, parents should be careful not to be pushy or overzealous. Due to their age, children need to be guided, encouraged and provided with platforms in which they can discover their special abilities.

Parents who notice a special ability in their children should find a balance between coercion and encouragement for their children to be stymied. Determining your child's degree of skills and level of interest will dictate where the balance will be placed.

Recognizing and nurturing talent

Recognizing Talent

Judging from the type of activities that your children find interest in, it is possible to determine the line of their talents and skills. Children who prefer creative tasks mostly have artistic skills, and you can support them by availing art materials for the purposes of their creative outlet. However, the choice of the art materials should correspond to the children's age, and you should avoid hazardous or toxic materials.

For children with musical talents, you will notice that they are always at ease or jovial when near any sound making appliances. They sing the right notes or discern tunes at a tender age. The talent in these kids can be recognized and nurtured by facilitating their exposure to different kinds of music. That is advantageous to both the talented and the non-talented. Therefore, parents should avoid being pushy.

Your child may also showcase comic or stage performing characteristics. That can be seen if they repeatedly try to imitate a certain lead character in a drama film or tell jokes over lunch or dinner. At times, you may find your child dressed up to imitate a particular actor he/she saw in a TV series, theater/film or even in the school drama club. You should support the child to build his/her confidence and self-esteem, and this improves the child's talent.

Regular bonding with sports equipment depicts that a child is deeply into sports. Physical activity should be your children's outlet if they have a habit of watching a game or playing with the ball. These talents can be recognized by buying the child sports equipment, visiting live games and hooking up your child to a team. If the child has a high interest in sports, you can consider referring them to a sports workshop in the neighborhood.

Nurturing Talent

Any new and upcoming talent that is not nurtured through the right channels will eventually die. Therefore, the need to look for professionals such as talent mentors and managers to nurture your child's talent in their early age arises. Always remember to 'make hay while the sun shines'. You should, however, be sensible in your decision and consider what your child desires and needs. The interest might be short-term and, therefore, you should be cautious before investing both your time and money. Ensure that there is longevity in the interest before making any serious move and do not pressure the child to please you.

Find an expert who will provide the right atmosphere for your child's talent to cultivate in. Above all, make sure that your child develops the inner satisfaction independent from external approval. Try as much as possible not to misinterpret your children's desires this will give room for their talents to blossom.

For more information on recognizing children's talents at an earlier stage visit the links below:

http://www.kidsource.com/kidsource/content4/special.talents.html

http://www.gifted.uconn.edu/nrcgt/reports/trifolds/a9818.pdf

Chapter 3: Helping children develop diverse skills

Parent are the most important and first teachers for their children. Children often learn social skills and behavior from their parents. Although it goes unsaid, each passing day, as a parent, you teach your child new ways of behaving, skills and information. Teaching for most parents comes naturally whereas others have to undergo training on how to teach skills to their children.

Methods of helping your child develop diverse skills

There are some ways and strategies in which you can help your children develop diverse skills as listed below:

Teaching by giving instructions

Giving instructions, in this case, means teaching a child by explaining what and how to do something. In most cases, you find yourself providing explanations and instructions to have disabilities and them, therefore, find difficulties in receiving and analyzing instructions perfectly. It is among the most efficient and easiest method to learn a new thing for a majority of children. However, in certain circumstances, it may not be the case since there are children who

Teaching by Showing

It can also be referred to as modeling. Children often and closely learn from what and how they see their parents do things. They learn and abide by their parent's style and approach to various issues. As a parent, you should, therefore, emulate the behaviors and skills that you would want your children to possess because they learn from you first-hand. Strive to be your children's role model. Teaching through modeling has proven to be the most successful way of helping children develop diverse talents compared to giving instructions.

Modeling is also suitable for demonstrating other useful behaviors and skills such as interaction with others. It can also be applicable in demonstrating a wide range of subtle ways of communication, for example, tonal variation and body language.

Teaching by approximations

Also known as shaping, this approach is guided by a very simple rule. It is a process to learn new behavior and skills. The very first attempts will only be similar to the end-result. For example, a child may pronounce certain words in an unclear manner that has been preceded by much worse pronunciations. However, the parents respond positively and enthusiastically each time the child tries to say the words. With time, the earlier versions of the child's pronunciations receive little reaction and attention and the parents helps to shape the child's pronunciation until it gets clear.

Teaching with procedures

It involves step-by-step teaching. There are activities and tasks that are too complex and require that you teach your child in a sequence of actions. You can simplify the learning process by breaking down the activity into smaller and easy steps. Ensure that your child is conversant with the first step and can do it without supervision before commencing the next step. Teaching with procedures is the most appropriate way of teaching a child to deal with the complicated tasks.

When helping children to develop diverse skills, irrespective of the method you apply, ensure that your children have a mastery of what you've taught them. Teaching the basic skills is the first step in helping a child to solve even the most complicated tasks. Supply them with the necessary and essential tools required to do as you ask.

Chapter 4: Ways to enhance children's cognitive and learning ability

Enhancing cognitive and learning ability in children is the progressive building of children's learning skills. The learning skills include thinking, memory, and attention. These essential and basic skills make children able to solve the sensory information and later learn to make comparisons, evaluate, remember and analyze. Besides a few cognitive and learning skills development being associated with the genetic makeup of the child, most cognitive and learning skills are learned. It means that you can enhance your children's cognitive and learning ability by giving them training.

To complete an academic activity successfully, a child requires efficient underlying and strong learning abilities. Cognitive skills help to process information correctly, and therefore children find school work easy and enjoyable to do. For these children, extra homework, special attention or school work particularly addressing underlying cognitive and learning skills prowess intensifies the ease of reading and learning.

Unfortunately, most learning institutions do not budget finances or the time to offer the relevant face-to-face training that best suits children with weak cognitive and learning abilities. Also, educators are authorized to teach at a speed that is difficult for children with underdeveloped cognitive and learning abilities to process and assimilate. It thus forces such students to lag behind academically as opposed to their peers and experience reading problems and learning difficulties. They tend to suffer a long-term series of learning struggles and fall further behind compared to their colleagues. Fortunately, this chapter provides ways to enhance children's cognitive function and learning ability as follows:

Allowing them enough sleep

Allowing your children, enough sleep is vital to their cognitive and learning abilities. Enough sleep has been scientifically proven to consolidate memory and learning. Consolidating learning is an intensive activity and, therefore, allowing the brain enough time to benefit from sleep is essential; there are fewer new inputs, availability of more energy and fewer distractions. No one should ever mislead you that sleep is a waste of time. Also, during sleep there are distinct roles that the two brainwave oscillations play, and these suggest the brain's extent of reorganization. Surprisingly, poor quality of sleep affects the gray matter volume in the frontal lobe and the entire brain as a whole.

Engage them in Brain-Training Games

It is very crucial to engage your children in brain-training games that involve handling multiple tasks as it will significantly boost their cognitive and learning skills. Today, scientists have a better understanding of the link between memory and learning and the specific technique of how spikes, patterns of electrical pulses, trigger numerous changes in various neutral circuits.

Engaging them in physical activities

Engaging your children in physical activities is a significant way of enhancing their cognitive and learning ability. According to the evidence discovered in a research at Boston University School of Medicine, physical activity helps to enhance brain cognition and health. This is because there is a significant increase in specific hormones during exercises that improve the brain memory. The researchers also from the same university correlated the hormone levels in the blood from aerobic fitness; they discovered that exercises were beneficial to the memory.

During endurance exercise, there is a specific molecule released that avoids degeneration of the brain and improves the cognitive brain function. The specific molecule is released in a chain reaction when exercising and is known as irisin. The hormone has neuroprotective effects, and its levels in the blood can be artificially increased to activate genes associated with learning and memory.

It is clear that optimizing your children's cognitive and learning abilities lies in the day-to-day exercises and habits. These habits help to flex all the two hemispheres of the brain cerebrum. The three habits mentioned above significantly enhance the child's cognitive function and prevent them from cognitive decline.

Chapter 5: Helping children understand human emotions of generosity and empathy

To some extent, human beings are naturally wired to be generous and empathetic. Approximately, all children in their younger years portray a generous and selfless behavior. According to Jane Nelsen who is a child therapist, "children are not capable of developmentally understanding empathy. However, that does not dictate that you should refrain from teaching it to them. You should not expect your teachings to have an immediate kick to your child.

Steps of helping your child understand these emotions

Helping children understand generosity and empathy may take part in two steps:

Labeling of Feelings

Helping children understand emotions in general is one of the basic steps in teaching them generosity and empathy. Similar to adults, children also experience all kinds of emotions from sadness to disappointment to frustration. However, contrary to adults, children do not have the experience in identification and management of those emotions. As a parent, you should regularly aid your children in naming their feelings and that will help them have a clear sense of their emotions.

A parent is the best emotional tutor of a child and they should help them understand the emotions of generosity and empathy at their young age. With time, your child will be able to understand the importance of generosity and empathy and how they affect those around them. As the children grow older, you should evolve the coaching from helping them understand their emotions to teaching them how to respond to their feelings.

Modeling Empathy

Another powerful way of teaching and helping children understand human emotions of generosity and empathy is by being empathetic and generous yourself. You should always try to be patient and calm with your children whenever they misbehave. Try as much as possible not to hit or yell at your children when they misbehave because it is not beneficial and helpful at all. That will only teach them that it is acceptable to yell or hit someone that has hurt their feelings and can lead them to doing unthinkable things to their peers.

Being concerned in your children's experiences and listening to them when they talk can also instill empathy in them. Also, you can also ask them questions and reflect on their answer as that will help them identify their feelings and thoughts. Modeling empathy and generosity has a way of incorporating those emotions to your children easily. Feelings of empathy and generosity enable your children to relate with others deeply. Your children will also improve in their ability to understand and act on empathetic and generous feelings by learning to help others, provide a listening ear and be generous.

You can visit the links given below for more information on the subject topic:

http://educationnorthwest.org/sites/default/files/developing-empathy-in-children-and-youth.pdf

http://magazine.byu.edu/?act=view&a=1960

Chapter 6: Helping children develop independent thinking early on

The thinking level in adults is at a higher dimension compared to that of children. It is, therefore, important to be patient with your child when you find that they have not done a job that they were supposed to have completed by the time you come back. According to an adult's perspective, these simple jobs usually seem regular and monotonous. On the other hand, these presumed simple jobs most children find them to be challenging, strenuous and humungous.

Children are supposed to master (from home) a wide range of skills and criteria before leaving for their higher studies. Developing independent thinking skills for children at an early age is essential and helps to build self-esteem and confidence in them. Toddlers and young children usually have interests in handling understandable and meaningful "adult-type" jobs. However, besides their enthusiasm, they lack skills and methods to handle these jobs. Create a congenial physical environment for your children that will greatly help them become more independent. A child can develop independent thinking early on if there is:

1. Provision of ample opportunities

You can help your child develop independent thinking early on by providing numerous opportunities for them to learn skills of independent thinking. Help them to understand the importance and benefits of independent thinking skills. Such benefits include increased efficiency and empowerment in and out of the class. Handling simple tasks with the child's initiatives is very beneficial to them and helps them carry out even more tasks that are straightforward and simple.

2. Showing flexibility

Giving room for flexibility towards your children is another way of helping them think independently. Although becoming independent is a slow process and takes time, it is important to respect the natural limitations of your child. Avoid putting pressure on them beyond the limits. Always integrate your work's ambit with the training. Make use of the time you have to train your children skills of independent thinking.

3. Allowance for children to work independently

Children often try to do simple tasks independent and free from supervision. Although they may do the first few attempts imperfectly, which is natural, always give them time to master the coordination of their brain and body parts. Let them try the tasks uninterruptedly.

4. Reinforcing positive assertions affirmatively

Always avoid reinforcing negative assertions. Teach them to be positive in life by being positive yourself. If they successfully handle a task, give them positive compliments from your heart. Below are some skills of independent thinking that you can help your child develop. However, the most important factor is to help your children understand the importance of independent thinking in achieving critical goals.

- Stress the importance of asking and answering questions with their efforts

- Encourage your child to always consider both sides of the coin before making decisions

- Encourage your children to often find their answers and solutions to problems

- Teach your children to do things by experimentation until they reach a correct and valid solution.

N.B.: children who develop independent thinking early on are the most successful in life.

Chapter 7: Instilling good values along with discipline in learning

In the contemporary world, the academic qualifications and achievements of a child have been highly valued compared to the child's character. This has a negative impact of bringing up a society with literate individuals but with a highly immoral behavior. That, however, does not imply that you should stop stressing the academic performance of your child. But you should remember that the true goal of education is knowledge coupled with character.

Most experts in childhood education recommend instilling of good values and discipline in children at a tender age. This is because, at this age, it is easy for children to be shaped and adapt to new values and discipline taught to them and live a value-filled life. Children easily emulate and adopt new lifestyles. Therefore, you should take advantage of that by instilling good values and discipline in them.

Instilling these values can be effective only under the following circumstances:

a) Cultivate a warm relationship

When children feel close to either or both of their parents, they are more willing to internalize and accept parental values. Also, families that are close usually share values and interests that reinforce each person.

b) Nurture an open communication

Having an open, honest and frequent communication with your children, especially the teens, is a catalyst of internalizing their parent's values. This gives the children a sense of dependency and makes them comfortable to talk to their parents about value-themed issues. An open communication enables you to understand your child's thinking perspective and you can appropriately advise them on good values. It also increases the odds of your child listening and incorporating your values. By nurturing an open communication, it is much easier to instill good morals and discipline to your children.

c) Give appropriate independence to your child

It is possible for children to initiate their principles, values and discipline by allowing them to practice necessary power in their lives. Giving your child several choices or setting them as unique individuals enables them to internalize good personal values and discipline. Again, it prevents them from pushing away with the aim of growing their sense of individuality.

d) Provide appropriate guidelines

Providing appropriate structures, guidelines and information that positively influence a child's decision-making is vital. It is paramount to set fair and clear expectations and follow the consequences as a way of instilling good values and discipline in your children. That, however, should be done with moderation. The consequences should not appear to be dictatorial as they will arouse feelings of rebelliousness, especially among the teens.

e) Cultivate practical skills

Initiating skills that put values learned into practice helps to build the self-confidence and esteem in both children and teens. Hence, they can internalize the values without fear or doubt. Also, building resistance and assertive skills and putting them into action reinforces positive values.

Chapter 8: Contribution of a learned child to a progressive nation

In today society, illiteracy has been a leading factor to the increased poverty index in various nations. It is, therefore, important to provide basic and secondary education to a child as that will be a massive contribution to the development of a progressive nation. Progressive education was established a few centuries ago and by contrast, it has found its way and roots in present experience.

Almost every progressive education program has certain common qualities. A learned child makes several contributions to a progressive nation such as:

- Progressive education emphasizes on expeditionary learning or learning by experimenting. Therefore, a child who has undergone this learning program grows up to be a highly proactive and a working individual. Thus, helps to build and develop his/her nation.

- Progressive education has an integrated curriculum that concentrates on thematic units. Such a system enables a child always to work with a theme or a purpose, thereby, contributing to the achievement of a nation's goal or objectives.

- There is an integration of entrepreneurship into the curriculum. Entrepreneurship skills enable a child to be innovative and creative by establishing new resources or improving the available resources. That helps to raise the living standards of individuals in a country.

- Also, progressive education emphasizes on critical thinking and problem solving. A learned child with these basic skills can achieve certain critical goals with ease and perfection. Children that possess these skills can give advice in a democratic nation on certain social issues.

- Most learned children who have undergone progressive education have skills in the development of social skills and group work. That enables the child to work comfortably in a team and work for the overall benefit of the society.

- In progressive education, children undergo various cooperative and collaborative learning projects. That enables a learned child to work in future without wrangles with the ruling authorities.

- Children also undergo various educational programs in democracy and social responsibility. That enables them to grow and build their esteem, and they can freely and boldly express their views on certain issues. They may end up giving significant advice and solutions that may benefit their society and the nation at large.

- Children who have undergone progressive learning are discouraged from dependency on textbooks and encouraged to embrace varied learning resources. This has the effect of enhancing independent thinking and improving the child's cognitive skills. Therefore, the child grows to become a problem solver in a nation.

Chapter 9: Distractions children face due to technology and lack of ambition

Distractions caused by technology

In the modern day society, there have been numerous inventions made in the technology sector due to the advancements in technology. In the high-tech classrooms, teachers and students have embraced the pros of using integrated tweets for presentations, using iPods and smart TVs during class. The pros of incorporating technology in schools include:

✓ Increasing interactions among students

✓ adding diversity to the lessons

✓ helping to bring in new knowledge and perspectives to students

Besides its many advantages, technology has negatively impacted the children's concentration due to the distractions they cause when inappropriately used. Laptops, video games, and iPods are among the common things that cause distraction to children either at home or in school. Technology negatively affects children in different ways as mentioned below.

Changing the thinking perspective of children

Technology has a way of changing a child's brain and how they think. It has been scientifically proven that the actual brain wiring can be altered by the continued use of technology. According to statistics, a small percentage of young children use mobile data. However, the percentage increases directly proportional as the children age. The prolonged usage of technology not only offers newfangled methods of doing things but also transforms their entire brain work. Video games, for example, have the effect of reducing a child's memory and increasing distractions.

Changing children's feelings

The ability to empathize in a child can be affected by the usage of technology. Children with less or no access to technological or electronic devices have a higher probability of picking up on emotions than those that have access. Prolonged use of technology also has the effect of changing a child's mood. It is a fact that children with less physical contact with their peers might face challenges in developing emotional reactions and social skills.

Putting children's safety and privacy at risk

Overuse or inappropriate use of technology makes a child vulnerable to plenty of risks. Children may unwittingly put themselves in danger while using technology either by posting or sharing certain information. In a majority of the online sex crimes that are against the children, the offenders acquired information on online social networking sites about the child's (victim) preferences. Online cyber-bulling has also been on the increase due to the anonymity of technology. Bullying among the teenagers is common by way of internet or texts.

Leads to Obesity

Prolonged usage of technology without engaging yourself in physical activities such as exercising may lead to obesity. Childhood obesity is gradually increasing courtesy of usage of technology. Obesity is also on the rise among the youth. For a long time, obesity was associated with the type, and the amount of food children eat; however, you should also control your children's usage of technology.

Distractions caused by lack of ambition

Ambition is what drives a person to work harder even when the environment is not favorable. Although it might sound ironic, working with an ambition is much more important than just working for a living. An ambitious person remains focused every time.

However, lack of ambition comes with it several distractions. A person without ambition in life can easily be manipulated into doing things that are vices in the society. Drug abuse is also caused by lack of ambition because most of the time you find yourself idling around.

For more on distractions caused by lack of ambition, technology and lack of motivation, visit the link below:

http://affirmyourlife.blogspot.com/2009/09/causes-for-lack-of-motivation.html

Note: it is important to check regularly your child's usage of technology and if possible set an appropriate time-limit for them. Also, you should advise your child and help them understand the benefits of living an ambitious life. However, this should be done with moderation.

Conclusion

We appreciate you so much for downloading this book and sparing time to read through it. Hopefully, this book has been of massive help to you as a parent in identifying ways of bringing up an ambitious child with good etiquette, values and discipline. By now it is clear to you that you can only influence your child's ambition but not make them the copyright of what you want them to be.

The next step is to adjust your parenting styles and avoid being dictatorial to foster independent and creative thinking in your child. Always remember that ambition is only a path to success but it is persistence that takes you there.

Finally, if you enjoyed and found this book informative, kindly do this favor, please leave a review on Amazon for this book. It'd be such an honor and greatly appreciated!

www.ingramcontent.com/pod-product-compliance
Lightning Source LLC
Chambersburg PA
CBHW070759180526
45168CB00004B/1678